Time to

Written by Jo Windsor

This animal can sleep in a den.

fox

This animal can sleep in a den, too.

bear

This animal can sleep in a tree.

koala

This animal can sleep
in a tree, too.

sloth

This animal can sleep in the water.

hippo

This animal can sleep in the air!

bird

Index

Guide Notes

> **Title: Time to Sleep**
> **Stage:** Emergent – Magenta
>
> **Genre:** Nonfiction (Expository)
> **Approach:** Guided Reading
> **Processes:** Thinking Critically, Exploring Language, Processing Information
> **Written and Visual Focus:** Photographs (static images), Index, Labels
> **Word Count:** 44

FORMING THE FOUNDATION

Tell the children that this book is about the different places animals sleep.
Talk to them about what is on the front cover. Read the title and the author.
Focus the children's attention on the index and talk about the different animals that are in this book.
"Walk" through the book, focusing on the photographs and talk about the different places that the animals are sleeping.

Read the text together.

THINKING CRITICALLY

(sample questions)

After the reading
- Why do you think animals find different places to sleep?
- What places do you think are the best to sleep in and why?

EXPLORING LANGUAGE

(ideas for selection)

Terminology
Title, cover, author, photographs

Vocabulary
Interest words: sleep, den, tree, water, air
High-frequency words: this, can, in, a, the
Positional word: in